TIME TRAVELERS

GREENLAND
MUMMIES

Janet Buell

Twenty-First Century Books
Brookfield, Connecticut

Twenty-First Century Books
A Division of The Millbrook Press, Inc.
2 Old New Milford Rd.
Brookfield, Connecticut 06804

Library of Congress Cataloging-in-Publication Data
Buell, Janet.
Greenland mummies / Janet Buell.
p.   cm.—(Time travelers)
Includes bibliographical references and index.
Summary: Describes the discovery of mummies in Greenland in 1972 and the work
of forensic anthropologists who investigated the remains of these members of the
Thule culture, ancestors of today's Eskimos.
ISBN 0-7613-3004-6
1. Inuit—Greenland—Juvenile literature. 2. Mummies—Greenland—Juvenile literature.
3. Thule culture—Greenland—Juvenile literature. 4. Forensic anthropology—Juvenile literature.
[1. Inuit—Greenland 2. Eskimos—Greenland 3. Mummies. 4. Forensic anthropology.
5. Greenland—Antiquities.] I. Title. II.Series.
E99.E7B83   1998   97-15231
998.2—dc21   CIP
                                                                                          AC

Designed by Kelly Soong
Map by Jeffrey L. Ward

Printed in the United States of America
1   3   5   4   2

Photo Credits

Cover photograph courtesy of Greenland National Museum & Archives.

Photographs courtesy of Greenland National Museum & Archives: pp. 8, 10, 16, 19, 30, 31, 47;
AP/Wide World: p. 15; Gamma Liaison: pp. 22 (© Pierre & Fred Vernay), 39 (© Theo Westenberger);
Woodfin Camp & Associates: pp. 24 (© John Eastcott/Yva Momatiuk), 27 (© Cynthia Haas), 33 (both
© John Eastcott/Yva Momatiuk), 34 (© Chris Bonington; Animals Animals: p. 25 (top © Owen
Newman, bottom © John Eastcott/Yva Momatiuk); © British Museum: p. 37; Canadian Museum of
Civilization: p. 43.

For my good friend,
Alan DeCosta

ACKNOWLEDGMENTS

Many thanks to Hans Grønvold and Jens Peder Hart Hansen. Thanks also to my editor, Pat Culleton, and to all the people at Twenty-First Century Books who have made bookmaking such an enjoyable experience.

CONTENTS

ONE
A STONY GRAVE

It was the perfect day for bird hunting in western Greenland, the largest island in the world. In the deep shadow of a stone mountain, twenty-year-old Hans Grønvold looked down at the shifting black waters of the fjord. To his left, the hulking mass of a rock ledge blocked the view of the summit. Behind and below him, Qilakitsoq lay nestled in a cove between the sheltering walls of the mountain.

Hans and his brother, Jokum, had come to Qilakitsoq since they were children, and they still loved the cold and wild edges of the ancient Arctic settlement. The two men claimed as ancestors a group of people who were among the first to inhabit the island, most of which lies above the Arctic Circle. Though outsiders once called them Eskimos, the Inuit prefer their word for themselves, which means "the People."

Early Inuit families used Qilakitsoq as a winter encampment. After centuries of use, they eventually abandoned it, and now only a few stones of their tent rings remain between the walls of the sheltered cove. On this October day, as Jokum and a few friends went ahead, Hans lagged behind. His slow pace allowed him time to notice things such as the odd arrangement of rocks piled beneath a ledgy outcropping.

Without thinking, Hans raised one of the rocks. As he did, his eyes widened

Hans Grønvold found the burial site of ancient Inuit mummies to the left of this Greenland fjord. At one time, Inuit families had a winter encampment here.

with surprise. There, wrapped in animal skins, lay a mummified human corpse. He removed other stones, revealing more corpses in the stony grave. Hans ran to fetch his brother and their hunting companions.

Later, in a letter to a friend, Hans described the scene:

"I...realized that I had found a grave which had never been opened before. There was a half-grown child lying on top, close to what was probably its mother, and then we saw a doll which had fallen to the side, a doll which turned out to be a little child. We put them back in place, with the child to the very back, by the rock. Only the eyes and the mouth of the child were damaged; everything was dried up."

The men lifted more rocks and soon found another chamber next to the first. Inside the second grave they could see a young woman who wore a beautiful fur outfit. Below her lay another corpse and beneath that one, another. Animal skins and high leather boots surrounded the bodies.[1]

A SECRET KEPT

The discovery excited Hans. Arriving home, he went directly to his bookshelves and searched through books on the history of the Inuit. He discovered no pictures that matched what he saw, but from the type of clothing they wore he suspected the bodies had been buried for at least one hundred years.

Hans reported the find to local police. They, in turn, forwarded the information to the Greenland National Museum. Radio programs discovered the story and broadcast news of it throughout the country. People called Hans and tried to convince him to lead them to the gravesite. He refused. Before they left Qilakitsoq that day, he, his brother, and their friends had made a pact, and Hans meant to keep it. He would not reveal the location until archaeologists could examine the bodies.

Hans waited eagerly for someone from the museum to call. No response. He sent a letter explaining what he'd found. He sent photographs and a map. Those, too, were met with silence.

You can imagine how he felt. Hans's family had lived in Greenland for generations, since the first Inuit skin boats touched the shores of the island. He couldn't understand why museum officials ignored this bone-and-flesh chance to learn more about his country's history.

Years passed, and Hans often returned to Qilakitsoq. Each time he did, he checked the graves, sure it would be the last time he would see the mummies. He knew treasure hunters seek out the riches and curiosities of old burial sites. It was only a matter of time before they would find the graves and take away the bodies.

Still, no one from the museum came.

Finally, in 1977, five years after his discovery, Hans decided to try one more time. He made the long trip to the Greenland National Museum, located in the

*A mummy wrapped in animal skins was revealed
when the top layer of rocks was removed.*

country's capital, Nuuk. There, he asked to see the photographs he had sent so
long ago. A clerk retrieved the folder, which had been filed away and forgotten.

As Hans looked at the snapshots, Jens Rosing, the museum's new director,
happened to pass by. Hans showed the director his pictures, and as he did, he

10

noticed excitement in Rosing's eyes. The director could immediately see the difference between this grave site and the other, usually skeletal remains, sometimes found in the Arctic.

Flesh still clothed these old Qilakitsoq bones. The photographs clearly showed their warm parkas, the burial furs, and their beautiful animal-skin boots, called kamiks. Rosing knew that Hans had stumbled upon something truly remarkable.[2]

In 1972, three Inuit hunters discovered the body of a woman that had washed out of a low beach cliff. A medical investigation showed that her face had been crushed and that she had inhaled moss particles. Scientists believe the woman suffocated to death after being trapped in her semi-subterranean house. It may have collapsed either from a landslide or earthquake.

MUMMIES IN THE GRAVES

Hans and Jokum had taken good care of the graves. When Rosing finally traveled to Qilakitsoq, he couldn't believe what he discovered within them. The child, which Hans had mistaken for a doll, was even more haunting and exquisite than its picture.

Though its spirit was long gone, its little body remained, and the dry weight of it pressed against the palms of Rosing's hands. He could imagine him a squirming, active baby. Beneath the fur edge of his parka hood, dark hair whisped across the little boy's forehead. His tiny, dried fingers curled from beneath his sleeves. Empty, lash-fringed eye sockets stared out from his sweet face.

Rosing found another body beneath the baby. It, too, was a child, but a few years older than the infant. It lay on top of a mummified adult, and wore a fur parka and pants.

Rosing knew there were more corpses buried in the stony graves, but he took only the two children and some of the loose animal skins buried with them. When he arrived home, he sent the bodies and skins to a laboratory in Denmark. There, they would be carbon-dated, a method that helps archaeologists determine the age of ancient things.

Three months passed before results of the carbon-dating tests arrived on the director's desk. As he read the report, Rosing's heart thumped with excitement. The people in the grave had died more than five hundred years earlier, making them the oldest and best-preserved humans ever discovered in the Arctic. Without Hans Grønvold's persistence, the bodies might have been lost forever.

Rosing and his team returned to Qilakitsoq, where they retrieved the rest of the corpses. Six more bodies filled the two stone chambers, as well as more than seventy fur skins and kamiks, which had been offered as grave goods to the dead Inuit.[3]

DETOUR TO DECAY

When most people hear the word *mummy*, they think of Egyptian mummies. Unlike ancient Egyptians, humans had no hand in turning these Arctic bodies into mummies. Nature did. To know why the Inuit bodies survived the decay process, you have to understand living organisms called bacteria. If you've ever had an upset stomach, strep throat, or earache, you've probably experienced an unwelcome invasion of these tiny, microscopic organisms. Like it or not, they assault your body every day. Most often you're strong enough to fight off a bacterial infection, but sometimes you're not. That's when you get sick.

Bacteria have a permanent home inside your body, too. These bacteria are the friendly kind that live in your gut, where they help digest the food you eat. The healthier you are, the better your chances of keeping a good supply of these useful organisms.

People with a lot of fat on their bodies decay quicker, too. Fat acts as insulation, and helps trap heat inside the body. Coverings of clothing or dirt create the same environment. The decaying process does not happen overnight. Under ordinary circumstances, it takes ten years for adult human tissue to decay totally. For children, it takes about five years.

Things change when the body dies. The heart no longer pumps blood, which delivers nourishment and oxygen to the organs and their cells. Without blood, the cells quickly weaken and die. The digestive enzymes that once helped break down food now start to eat through the stomach and intestines. You can think of this process, called autolysis, as the body digesting itself.

As the body dies, bacteria grow out of control. Organisms that once lived in the airways and stomach migrate through veins and arteries. As they go, they feast on blood and tissue. Bacteria living outside the body enter to help with the job.

This process, which scientists call putrefaction, makes dead bodies decay. It is not pleasant to think about, but we should be grateful that it happens. If it didn't, our world would be piled high with animals that died only yesterday, those that died thousands of years ago, and all the years in between.[4]

FREEZE-DRIED BODIES

The ancient bodies lasted so long because special circumstances created a natural decay detour. The Qilakitsoq people died in a cold climate, which slowed the work of bacteria. Though the organisms can live in cold temperatures, they thrive in warmer ones. One example of this is the way bacteria work in someone who dies with a high fever. Bacteria multiply quickly in the heat of fevered tissue, so a warm body decomposes faster than a cooler one.

The Qilakitsoq people may have died in winter, which would have hampered bacterial growth more than usual. The tiniest of them probably cooled fastest, which was why, surprisingly, the infant looks so alive.

Like most living things, bacteria survive best when there's plenty of water. In this case, a rock overhang above the burial chamber kept the bodies very dry. The constant arctic wind helped further, working its way through holes in the rock walls, where it dried the corpses' skin. This combination of low temperatures and wind helped freeze-dry the ancient people in much the same way that modern food is freeze-dried.[5]

MYSTERIOUS MUMMIES

The number of corpses and the degree of preservation surprised the scientists. Never before had an Arctic burial site yielded such a wealth of ancient history.

There was mystery here, too. Who were the people discovered in these graves? Their burial chamber lay a distance from the ancient settlement they once inhabited. Who had brought their bodies to this faraway place? Were they from the same family? Did they die from a common accident? Or, did they die separately, to be buried one by one on this cold and lonely mountainside?

Rosing and his team knew there were ways to discover the secrets held within the stony graves. Over the last several years, scientists have developed an amazing number of tools that allow them to examine living people for diseases and other afflictions. Giving modern technology an ancient spin, these same tools would make it possible for the Greenland mummies to tell their story.

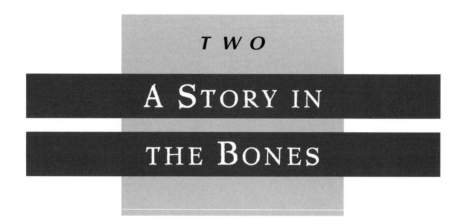

T W O

A STORY IN
THE BONES

Words are the way humans communicate, but it's not the only way. Look around and you can see what others are "saying," even if they're not speaking a word.

If your brother has his arms folded tightly across his chest, he's probably indicating he won't tell you which girl he likes best. Your teacher may not say she's angry, but if she has narrowed her eyes and placed her hands on her hips, it could mean you're in big trouble. This is body language. Ancient humans speak in a kind of body language, too, but it's not like the body talk living people use. The ancient dead speak to us in the language of bones, skin, hair, and teeth.

These things tell scientists a lot about humans of the past. An example of this is the *Mary Rose*, one of King Henry VII's battleships. The vessel sank in an English harbor in 1545 while on its maiden voyage. Archaeologists raised the ship from its watery grave in 1982, more than four hundred years after it sank.

The ship itself was a great find, made even more exciting by the discovery of a number of human skeletons within its hull. One of them was a man in his mid-twenties, who was making his way up to the main deck when the *Mary Rose* sank. A study of his bones showed that this man was likely an archer, a soldier who fights with a bow and arrow. Years of the twisting motion archers use to launch an arrow had worn the man's vertebrae in a particular way. His lower left arm bone, the ulna, had grown thick and worn from pushing on his bow.[1]

Modern equipment makes it possible for ancient vessels such as the Mary Rose, which sank in 1545, to be raised from the deep. The ship was placed in a cradle underwater, then transferred to a support frame and brought to shore on a barge.

X-Ray Visions

When flesh covers bone, as it does with the Greenland mummies, scientists use X rays to see them. X rays are light rays that can pass through some materials like wood and paper, but not through denser materials like metal. When technicians x-ray a human body, bones block some of the rays. The rays pass right through soft skin tissue where they strike a photographic plate and leave an image. In the photographic image, the contrast between soft and dense tissue shows up as a picture of the body's internal bony structure.[2]

The scientists found it wasn't easy to x-ray the mummies. Living humans are flexible, and usually do what they're told. The ancient Inuit weren't as cooperative. Their clothing was in beautiful condition, but as stiff as cardboard after years of burial. Some of the adults had been buried with their knees and necks bent.

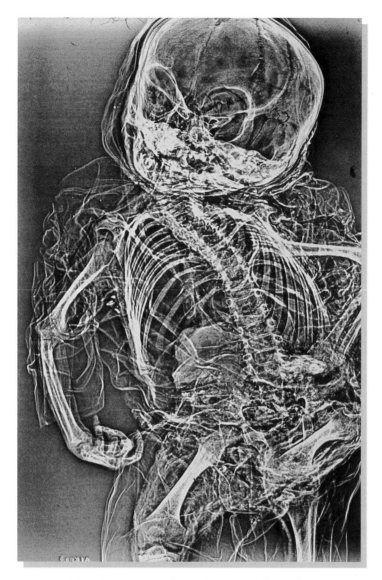

*Scientists x-rayed the mummies to help them
determine age, gender, and the possibility of disease.*

This made it difficult to fit them under the X-ray machine. With some clever maneuvering, the technicians finally managed to x-ray their unusual "patients."

The X-ray photographs gave scientists an inside view of the mummies' bodies. This view would help them complete their first task, which was to identify the ages and sexes of the eight ancient people.[3]

LONG BONES AND SUTURES

Forensic anthropologists are specialists in the human body. They're experts on the way a skeleton changes during an individual's life. And they understand the ways it has changed throughout human history.

They know, for instance, that human bones grow from the time we're born until we're about twenty years old. When a young person experiences a "growth spurt," a time of rapid growth, the long bones grow very quickly, adding bone tissue at their ends. As more tissue is added, growth lines develop where new bone grows onto old. A forensic anthropologist can "read" these growth lines to help determine the age of those bones.[4]

A forensic anthropologist also can look at a person's skull to tell its age. Your skull doesn't start out as one solid piece when you're born—it is made up of bony plates connected by soft tissue. Scientists call the places where these plates meet sutures. This flexible design allows the skull to expand as the brain grows. After the brain reaches full size, the tissue of the sutures begins to ossify, or turn to bone.

Scientists use X rays to see the development of sutures, which can help them determine a person's age. They can pinpoint an infant's age within two or three months of its actual age. They can tell the age of an older teenager to within a year.[5]

When scientists x-rayed the baby, which they called Mummy 1, they could see that his bones had been developing for six months. The way his teeth had developed helped confirm his age. X rays didn't tell them the youngest mummy's sex, but his clothes were of a style historians know Inuit boys wore around five hundred years ago.

X rays of the other child, named Mummy 2, showed that he was about four years old when he died. As with the baby, X-ray photographs couldn't help scientists determine if Mummy 2 was male or female. The only way they could tell was to remove its clothing, which they did. Beneath the fur parka and pants was a young boy.

X-ray photographs did show that Mummy 2 had surprisingly little calcium in his bones for a boy his age. Calcium is a mineral that gives bones their strength, so the young boy's bones would have been very brittle and weak. As they examined him, scientists discovered something else. The boy had a misshapen pelvis. The top ridges of the pelvic bone, which form the hips, had turned outward on each side. This abnormality told investigators that the boy probably had Down syndrome, a form of retardation that would have hampered his mental and physical development.[6]

If that weren't enough, the boy also had Legg–Calve'–Perthes disease, which had destroyed the top of his femur, the long thigh bone that fits into the hip socket. With his hip and leg problems, the young boy probably could not walk. Despite this, the boy's kamiks were very worn on their soles.

This discovery confused the scientists. It seems as though the boy's kamiks told one story, his bones another. Scientists wanted to know how a boy who couldn't walk created so much wear on the soles of his kamiks. Their best guess was that before they placed him in his grave, the boy's family traded his unworn kamiks for the worn kamiks of a living child. Somehow, when they exchanged the boots, they had put the left boot on the right foot, and the right boot on the left.[7]

GRAVE WOMEN

Forensic anthropologists know that as people grow older, the bones ossify more completely. This makes it harder for them to determine how old an adult is over a certain age. Sometimes they have only small clues to help solve the mystery. One clue might be the way arthritis has worn down the bones of the spine. Another might be the degree of wear on the teeth.

Mummy 5 proved to be an older woman, who was about fifty-five when she died. Scientists discovered that she, too, had very little calcium in her bones, which isn't unusual in a woman her age. The lack of calcium caused a few of the vertebrae in her spine to collapse. The woman probably experienced aggravating backaches from these collapsed vertebrae.

Scientists also use bones to tell if a person is male or female. The usual and quick way to tell a person's sex is to look at their unclothed bodies. Since they had already decided not to undress the four best-preserved mummies, scientists decided to use X rays to help them answer this question.

The scientists studied X rays of the bones carefully, to see if there were differences among the mummies. In many cultures, including ancient ones, men are often larger than women, and their bones are usually larger, too. Men have bonier skulls and a thicker browbone, called a supraorbital ridge. Often, the places where muscles attach to bone are larger in men than they are in women.

Scientists also can tell whether a person is a man or a woman by looking at the person's pelvis, the cradle of bone located between the hips. A man's pelvis is high and narrow. A woman's, on the other hand, is usually lower and wider, which allows a baby to pass through on its way to being born. Scientists can also tell if a woman has given birth or not. After she does, her pelvis develops a groove along its surface.[8]

Using bones to tell a person's sex isn't foolproof. Scientists thought X rays of Mummy 5 showed that he was a man. When they undressed him, however, they discovered he was actually a she. Scientists couldn't tell if Mummies 3 and 6 were male or female, but the cut of their clothing and tattoos on their faces suggested they were both women.

It appeared that all the adults in the grave were women. Mummy 3, who lay beneath the four-year-old boy, was a twenty-five-year-old woman. Mummy 4 was about thirty. Mummies 5, 6, and 8 were women over fifty years old.[9] Mummy 7 was between twenty-five and thirty years old.

Mummy 4 was about thirty years old when she died more than 500 years ago. Because she and the mummies found with her were buried in a cold, dry place, they were actually freeze-dried and were remarkably well preserved.

X rays also told scientists a lot about the ancient Greenlanders' health. X-ray photos of Mummy 8, a fifty-year-old woman, show that she fractured her clavicle, or collarbone, about a year before she died. If she had been alive today, a doctor would have immobilized her arm to give the clavicle time to heal properly. Mummy 8 didn't have this medical information, so she continued using her arm. This kept the bones from growing together again and probably made one arm weaker than the other one. It also ached until the day she died.

X rays give scientists the same information about dead humans as they do about living ones. X-ray photographs show bone fractures, both old and new. They also provide a picture of diseases that affect the skeletal system, such as leprosy and tuberculosis.

Scientists got an excellent, close-up view of Mummy 8's head because the skin connecting it to her body had disintegrated. X rays revealed that disease had eaten away bone at the base of her skull and at her left ear and eye socket. Scientists could tell the destructive disease was a type of head cancer, common even in the Inuit today. It probably caused her unbearable pain and made her blind in one eye. Despite this, the woman continued to work until her death. Scientists found evidence of cut marks from sinew thread on her thumbnail. This means she was still sewing garments until the end of her life.[10]

THREE
ANCIENT ARCTIC
DWELLERS

As good as science is, it can't tell us everything about the Greenland mummies. It can't, for example, tell us their names. And it can't tell us if one had a great singing voice or if another liked to roughhouse with her children. What we do know about their lives we know by studying the way people throughout history have adapted to the frozen extremes of our world.

The people who occupied those graves were members of the Thule culture, ancestors of the arctic dwellers we now call Inuit. To simplify things, we will use the term *Inuit* for this book. There is little that remains of the early Inuit of a thousand years ago, so scientists and historians study their descendants to understand what they were like. They feel there is strong evidence to show that the more modern Inuit, those that lived before extensive contact with Europeans in the 1800s, used many of the same survival methods developed by their ancient ancestors.

The Inuit most likely began their Arctic journey in Asia, crossing the Bering Strait to Alaska in their umiaks, large skin boats. From about A.D. 900 to 1100, they made their way through the Canadian Arctic and east to Greenland, hunting whales and other cold-water animals as they went.[1]

To those of us who live in lower latitudes, choosing to live in the frozen north seems like a strange thing to do. Most of us love summertime, which never seems to last quite long enough. And we like the days and nights of our world to pass in regular intervals once every twelve hours or so.

Life is different in the Arctic. In winter, when the North Pole tips away from the sun, the top of the world slips into continuous night. The sun sets in mid-October and doesn't rise again until mid-February. It's cold in the Arctic, too, sometimes unbearably so. January temperatures range from 14°F above zero to 30°F below. They sometimes plummet even more dangerously, to –80°F.[2]

Despite how snowy the Arctic seems to be, there is very little water in the snow that falls there. Frigid air can't hold as much water vapor as warm air can, which makes the Arctic as dry as California's Mojave Desert. The Arctic has lots of snow because so little of it melts or evaporates, making it hundreds or even thousands of years old in some places as the layers pile up.

Cold weather doesn't wait until winter. The northern oceans begin to freeze in autumn. The big freeze locks over 6 million square miles of ocean into a bleak and frigid whiteness. As the water freezes, wind and currents lift the ice into odd shapes and angles. The landscape becomes a mass of frozen ridges, mounds, and hills.

Traveling over this ice can be very difficult. Spring is one of the most treacherous times. When the thaw begins, the giant sheet of ocean ice, called pack ice, begins to fracture into smaller pieces, or floes. During spring breakup, it's not

Melting pack ice breaks into smaller floes when the spring thaw begins.

22

unusual for an unlucky traveler to find himself on one of these floes drifting helplessly out to sea.[3]

SHORT SUMMER, QUICK PLANTS

It doesn't seem possible that anything can live in such a cold and unwelcoming place. Even during its short summer season, the ground stays frozen. This frozen base, called permafrost, extends thousands of feet down and has stayed frozen for thousands of years. Only the top one to ten feet or so of topsoil ever defrosts in the Arctic.

Despite this, plants do grow on the vast expanse of Arctic plain called the tundra. There are trees here, but no towering forests. Trees need deep anchor roots to grow large, and roots can't penetrate rock-hard permafrost. The biggest trees, birches and willows, may be no bigger around than your finger. And though they're only a few inches high, they're likely to be hundreds of years old.

Only plants that have developed Arctic strategies can survive the short and cold growing season. Most of them grow close to the ground, where the dark soil absorbs warmth from the distant sunshine. This low-growing strategy also keeps them from drying out or tearing apart in the wind that blows relentlessly across the tundra.

With summer so short, plants need to grow and reproduce fast. And they do, much faster than their southern cousins. Some plants, such as *Geum glaciate,* can bloom before the snow has completely melted. A number of plants pollinate themselves, while others don't even need pollen to reproduce. Those plants needing insects for pollination attract them with colorful, fragrant blossoms. In the short Arctic summer, the tundra ignites with color. Yellow arctic poppies blaze in the summer sun, the white heads of shaggy-haired cotton grass sway above boggy hollows, while pink campions hug immense stretches of the chilly plain.[4]

SURVIVAL STRATEGIES

Like plants, humans need strategies to survive in such a cold and forbidding place. Food, water, and shelter are the main things humans need to survive. Here, it seems that none of these things are very easy to find.

When they were alive, the Greenland mummies didn't drive to the local grocery store for food. Instead, they needed to catch, clean, and prepare it. As you can imagine, this was a full-time job, especially in the dark months of winter.

During the short Arctic summer, the tundra comes alive with vibrant color.
The rest of the year, from September to April or May, it is usually covered with snow.

Fortunately, the land was full of hunting opportunities. Ringed seals, hooded seals, tusked narwhals, beluga whales, walruses, and arctic cod were, and still are, some of the animals that swam the Arctic seas. Feathered creatures populated the water and land: eider ducks, loons, snowy owls, arctic swans, puffins, kittywakes, and murres. Caribou, musk oxen, hares, and foxes roamed the wide, flat tundra.[5]

But these animals were cautious and didn't just stand around waiting to be killed. The Inuit had to develop clever ways to hunt these wary creatures.

If an Inuit hunter wanted to capture seals in summer, he would take to the sea in his kayak. A kayak is a one-person boat made of a bone frame and a waterproof sealskin covering. In this swift little boat, he'd approach a seal and hurl

*In spring and summer, snowy owls (top) raise young,
and caribou (bottom) graze on the plants.*

his harpoon at it. When the barbed blade of the harpoon pierced its skin, the seal dove to get away. As it did, the long throwing shaft separated from the blade and floated to the surface where the hunter retrieved it.

Attached to the harpoon blade was a rope, which was coiled loosely on the deck of the kayak. At the other end of this rope was an air-filled seal bladder. As the seal made its escape, it dragged the rope and bladder behind it. The air-filled bladder made it more difficult for the seal to swim. After a while, the hunter would see the bladder pop to the surface. That meant the seal was rising, too. When the hunter spied the bladder, he quickly paddled to the spot. As the seal surfaced for a breath of air, it would see the hunter and sink without taking it. After a time, the seal became too tired to keep swimming. Exhausted and out of breath, it floated to the surface, where the hunter struck a final blow with his spear.[6]

WINNING WINTER STRATEGIES

Hunting in the wintertime was even more difficult. In winter, the frozen seas forced the Inuit to leave their kayaks and hunt sea mammals through the ice.

First, the hunter had to locate an agloo, or breathing hole, made by seals and other sea mammals. Seals make these openings so they can rise just far enough through the ice to take a breath of air.

The next step was to wait patiently, harpoon poised and ready. Since seals keep more than one breathing hole, a hunter could wait for hours for one to surface at the hole where he was standing. It was tedious, tiring work. When a seal finally did rise, there were no second chances. The hunter needed an accurate and quick aim or he would lose the seal.

An Inuit hunter used imitation to stalk seals that had hauled up on the ice. Just like a seal, the hunter lay on the ice, raising his head to look around whenever the seal raised his. He also raised his feet and pressed them together to imitate the seal's flippers. Whenever the seal slept, the hunter edged closer to his prey. Stalking a seal in this way could take two or three hours.

Since agloos may be only a few inches across, the Inuit hunter had to use his ice ax to chop a bigger hole to raise the harpooned seal through the ice. As he did this, he held onto the harpoon rope tightly or tied it to his dogsled to keep the dead seal from slipping beneath the ice and out of his reach.[7]

Necessity: The Mother of Invention

Since there are so few resources in the Arctic, the Inuit had to be clever about using what little there were. They never hunted animals for sport. And they never wasted one bit of the animals they took. The skins of their catch were made into clothes, blankets, or coverings for kayaks and umiaks. The Inuit transformed the bladders and stomachs of animals into floats or storage containers. They used animal fat as lamp oil and as fuel to cook their food. They took bones and teeth and made strong tools out of them for the hunt or for other tasks.[8]

The dogsled is one example of the brilliance of Inuit ingenuity. The Inuit of Alaska assembled a sled frame out of bones, antlers, or driftwood. Then they would stretch seal or caribou skin over it. However, in Canada and Greenland, the Inuit preferred flat sleds made of wood or sometimes of whalebone. The sled's runners, the long bladelike strips it rides on, were cross-braced with caribou antlers and tied with sealskin ropes.

The Inuit of Greenland and Canada used a fan hitch to connect their dogs to a dogsled. As seen here, each dog was tied to the sled on a separate line, and the dogs fanned out in front of the sled to pull it.

The runners could be made of wood, ivory, or bone. On the bottom of the runners, the people layered a mixture of shredded moss and water, which turned to ice. Then they would smooth and shape another layer of ice on the runners, which would help the sled slip over the surface of snow or ice. Sometimes when other materials were scarce, the Inuit tightly wrapped a kind of trout, called char, head to tail in a wet sealskin and used it as runners. The sealskin would freeze hard enough to slide over the ice and snow. [9]

F O U R

KEEPING

WARM

The Inuit had to be just as clever when it came to battling bitter temperatures and biting arctic wind. They made special clothing to keep a hunter warm while he waited for prey to come within range and flexible enough for him to move quickly when it did. The clothing was also easily vented so the wearer could release excess body heat.[1]

Like other Inuit, the Qilakitsoq people knew that warm air trapped within layers of clothing was the best protection against cold. When scientists investigated the mummies' clothing, they found that the women had worn two layers of animal skin clothing. Their inner parkas, or jackets, were made of feathered bird skin. Layered feathers trap air, which kept the women as warm as they did the original owner. The women made their outer hooded parkas of sealskin and caribou skin. Tiny insulating air chambers honeycomb each shaft of caribou hair, making it one of the warmest, most lightweight furs in the world.[2]

The Inuit wore two pairs of trousers, or pants. In very cold weather, they wore long, outer pants. In summer, the women wore very short, tight trousers made of sealskin or caribou. Their kamiks, or boots, were so high they reached to the hem of their shorts and were ingeniously crafted. They were made out of sealskin, sewn with sinew thread that expanded slightly when wet. This made the seams of these boots as waterproof as the skins themselves. Inside their kamiks, the Inuit wore

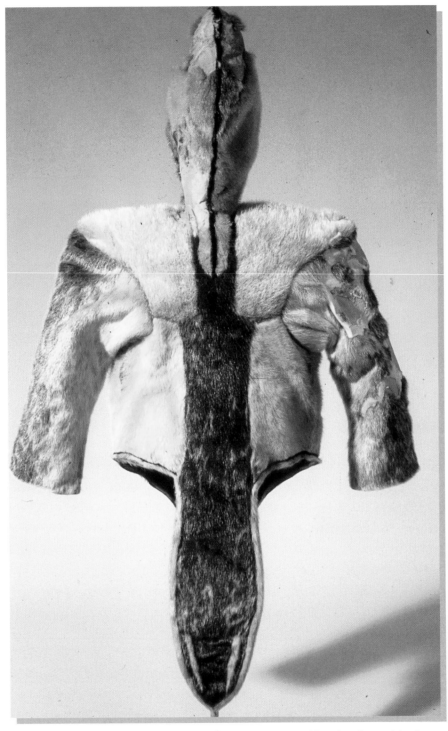

This anorak (seen from the back) was preserved by the dry cold of the grave, so it was relatively easy to restore it to its original shape.

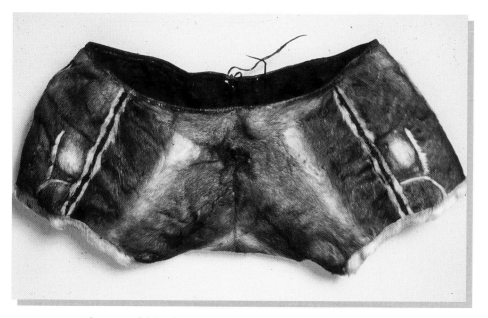

These sealskin shorts, although more than 500 years old, still show how skillfully the fur pieces were joined.

thin skin stockings. And between those two layers, they stuffed dried grass to provide extra insulation.[3]

Inuit women knew which skins worked best for their clothing. Caribou taken in the fall, before the animal's coat grew thick for winter, was lightest in weight and also very warm. Sometimes a woman soled her man's kamiks with polar-bear fur so he could walk quietly on the ice. Undergarments were constructed of bird skin or the soft skin of a caribou calf. Seal intestines provided the Inuit with waterproof rain clothing.[4]

Their clothing was so well-designed that only ten pounds of it could keep the wearer warm to –60°F for long stretches of time. Occasionally, it even acted as shelter. In some Arctic regions, a man on the hunt might sleep outdoors with nothing more than a windbreak made of snow. He would use his mittens to sit on and then pull his arms inside his parka, folding them across his chest. Falling over as he slept would release the warm air trapped within his parka, so the man braced himself by sitting forward with his arms against his knees. Inuit clothing was so perfect that until explorers like Robert Peary and Charles Francis Hall started using it, all attempts at Arctic conquests ended in failure.[5]

WOMEN'S WORK

In most Inuit families, the man and woman divided their duties. Men hunted and made tools, while women made clothing and did other domestic tasks.

Making clothing wasn't easy. To begin, the woman had to flense the animal, which means she cut away its skin and blubber. Next, she carefully scraped away all traces of blubber with her ulu, a crescent-bladed knife. After that, she soaked the skin in urine to remove any blubber that remained.

When the skin had soaked long enough, the woman stretched and dried it. She did this by cutting holes in the skin's edges and then putting pegs in the holes to pin it to the ground or to snow. The Qilakitsoq people did this, too. Scientists found peg holes on the edges of their skin clothing.[6]

Inuit women used tools to prepare the hides, including bone awls for punching holes, sewing needles of bone, ivory, or meteor iron, a skin ring used as a thimble, a bone for making the pleats at the toes of a kamik. Though the archaeologists found no evidence of these tools with the mummies' bodies, they discovered that the Qilakitsoq did use a tool that all Inuit women used for making clothing—that tool was their teeth.

Despite how difficult life was in the Arctic, Inuit women were surprisingly fashion-conscious. Their parkas were stylishly short, with high and narrow hoods. Some women made their parkas with long tails in the back. When they designed their short trousers, they made them with different colored fur and trimmed them with lighter-colored animal skins. Even though the weather in the Arctic was very cold, they often designed their clothing so that their arms and legs were exposed.

When she scraped a hide, an Inuit woman held one end of it between her teeth. After that, she rubbed the skin over her lower front teeth. To sew the garment, first she had to soften the hide's tough edges by chewing them.

Once it was made, clothing often stiffened as it dried overnight. Every morning, the woman chewed her family's garments and the soles of their kamiks to soften them.

She even used her teeth to make threads from animal sinew, a cord of dense, tough tissue that connects muscle to bone. First she split the thick sinew into thinner lengths with her ulu. Next, she rolled the sinew against her cheek and then pulled it between her teeth. After years of doing this, the woman's teeth developed grooves, or furrows, along their biting edges.

A modern-day Inuit uses an ulu (left) *to cut out sealskin boots. An Inuit woman* (right) *sews fur to an anorak in much the same way as her ancestors did.*

When dental specialists investigated the mummies' mouths, they discovered all but the youngest woman and the children had developed furrows on their front teeth. The stress of heavy chewing caused the roots of some of their teeth to shorten. Occasionally, they disappeared altogether. When they did, the teeth fell out. Scientists could tell which of the mummies' teeth were lost ante-mortem, which means before death, because skin had grown over the holes. Enamel, the hard outer coating of the tooth, had cracked on their remaining teeth.

After years of chewing animal skins, the women's teeth no longer resembled normal teeth. Instead, they looked like short, stubby pegs. Some of the older women's teeth were so short they most likely could not chew their food very well. Instead, they probably swallowed big chunks of it whole.[7]

A Warm Home

Most people think the Inuit lived in igloos year round, but that only happened in the central Arctic. Most often igloos, or inni as the Inuit called them, were temporary winter shelters.

Making an igloo required a great deal of skill, and both men and women undertook the task. First, the builders had to find the right kind of snow, the kind packed hard by the wind. Then they cut it into blocks of the right size and shape. Next, they layered the blocks in a spiral so they sloped inward and met at the top. Darkness, wind, and cold made the project even more difficult.

After they built the igloo, they packed snow into the chinks between the blocks to keep it snug in the wind. They sealed the house from the inside, too. A

It takes less than two hours to cut snow blocks and put them together to form an igloo.

small fire made the walls melt slightly. When the walls thawed enough, the builders extinguished the fire. The melted snow then froze again, sealing the room with a fine glaze of ice.

If the family planned to stay in their snow shelter longer than one night, they lined the walls with fur skins. Sometimes they constructed a window of clear sea ice to allow in sunshine. Inside, the bodies of the residents heated the igloo enough to keep it cozy and warm.

The common winter residence for most Inuit was made of stone, bone, and blocks of sod. In this case, the sod blocks were pieces of tundra cut and piled on top of the stone and bone framework. The builders insulated the house further by packing snow and ice around it. These sod homes were semi-subterranean, which meant they were partly underground, usually about three feet down.

To enter the house, residents crawled through a long, subterranean tunnel. The tunnel kept the house ventilated, but also kept heat, which rises, from escaping through the entranceway. The builders made a skylight near the top of their home, and covered it with translucent seal intestine. A smaller hole cut at the top allowed for more ventilation.

Before they entered their home, the Inuit brushed snow off their clothing so it wouldn't melt and make their garments and their home wet. Then they undressed and hung their clothes to dry. Most people in an Inuit family went naked inside their homes or wore briefs made out of animal skin.[8]

FROSTBITE

As good as these measures were, sometimes in extremely cold weather or biting wind, they just didn't work. Frostbite, which first reveals itself as white patches on the skin, was a constant danger. A lone traveler wrinkled his or her face often to feel for stiff areas that meant frostbite. Sometimes, all it would take to warm the skin was to place a warm hand over the spot.

There were times, however, when nothing could keep the skin from freezing. When that happened, blood couldn't get into the dead and dying tissue. Then a dangerous infection, called gangrene, would set in and spread to the rest of the body. Death was likely to follow unless the frozen limbs or toes were amputated. If the Inuit hunter was alone, he had to do the amputation himself. You can imagine the terrible results of frostbite, since the Inuit had no anesthetics to dull the pain or antibiotics to fight infections.[9]

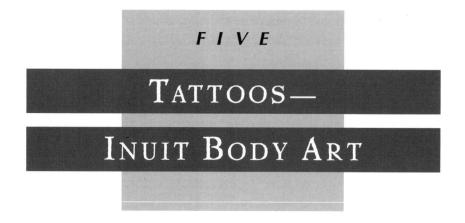

TATTOOS—
INUIT BODY ART

The Inuit didn't have a written language until the nineteenth century. Without one, it's hard to retrieve the facts behind their mysterious, distant history. To better understand their culture, scientists and historians turn to the writings of early visitors who first met the Inuit. These visitors were the European explorers and traders who traveled throughout Greenland and other Inuit territories from the sixteenth century to early in the twentieth century.

Sometimes these encounters had disastrous results for the Inuit. Outsiders carried diseases that Arctic people had never encountered. Since their bodies hadn't experienced these viruses and bacteria, the Inuit had not developed a resistance to them. Visitors brought smallpox, pneumonia, tuberculosis, measles, and influenza, which spread quickly through a village, killing large numbers of its population. An example of this devastation is what happened to the Sadlermiut people of Southampton Island, in Hudson Bay. The entire Sadlermiut nation became extinct in 1900 from the diseases brought by the crew of just one Scottish whaler.[1]

Encounters with outsiders were unpleasant in other ways, too. In the eighteenth century, Russian fur traders crossed the Bering Sea in search of fur and other valuables. In their quest for wealth, the Russians overhunted fur seals, sea otters, and foxes, leaving little for the Aleuts, distant relatives of the Inuit.

Not only did the Russians slaughter the Aleuts' main source of food, but the men often enslaved or murdered many of them. By 1766, 70 to 90 percent of the Aleuts had died from murder, mistreatment, disease, and starvation.[2]

Earlier, the English explorer Martin Frobisher traveled to the Arctic during expeditions in 1576, 1577, and 1578. There he first encountered "men in small boates made of leather." Frobisher's crew traded peacefully with the arctic residents until they decided to kidnap an Inuit man and his kayak, taking them back to England as specimens to study. On another expedition, Frobisher captured other "specimens" of arctic life: an Inuit man, woman, and child. The painter John White drew and painted pictures of these people. Eventually, all four captives died of pneumonia.

Many modern-day historians use White's pictures to compare Inuit

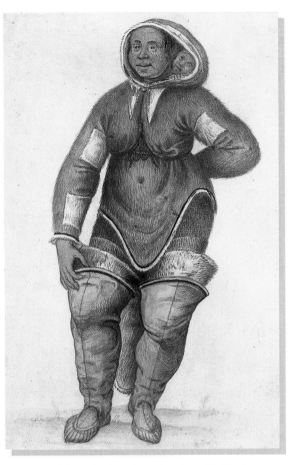

This painting from the late 1500s depicts an Inuit woman. Notice the small child peering from inside the hood.

fashion with that of the Greenland mummies. Like the women in the graves, the Inuit woman in White's painting wears a hooded fur parka. Her parka shows evidence of the same "tail" the Greenland mummies wore on their jackets. The woman's skin stockings protrude over the top of her kamiks.

The woman also wears tattoos on her face. Tattoos are permanent designs made by placing a coloring agent, called pigment, under the very top layer of skin. Historical evidence shows that tattooing was a common practice for the early Inuit and their descendants. Ancient human statues made by the Inuit show deep lines, which represent tattoos, carved on their faces.

An Inuit family, captured by Danish explorers in the 1650s, gives us one close-up view of this ancient custom. A painting made by a Danish artist depicts

Other Danish explorers captured nine Inuit and brought them back to Denmark. The Danes considered the Inuit a novelty. They took them to parties and made them wear fancy clothes that were popular with Europeans at the time. All nine Inuit eventually died, most of them from grief and homesickness. One died while pearl fishing in a fjord, another when he tried to return to Greenland in his kayak.

the family dressed in their fur clothing. The man holds the harpoon he used to spear fish and sea mammals. One woman holds a fish, and a young boy holds a dead seabird. Both women wear tattoos on their forehead, cheeks, and chin.[3]

HIDDEN TATTOOS

At first, scientists couldn't tell if the Greenland mummies wore tattoos. A heavy, white mold grew in a thick layer over the mummies' faces, hair, and clothing. The mold presented a problem for the scientists. In some people, certain molds can cause severe allergies. In others with weakened immune systems, it can cause death. Before they could work with the moldy bodies, the scientists needed to test the fungus to see if it was hazardous to humans. They eventually determined it was safe to work with and began removing it from the mummies.

As they removed the mold, scientists began to see evidence of tattoos on the women's faces. The evidence was much too faint to see clearly, so they decided to get a better look with a technique called infrared photography. Unlike the regular light rays we see with, infrared rays reach below the epidermis, which is the outer layer of skin. This allows a view of anything that may be hidden beneath it in the next layer, called the dermis.[4]

Under the warmth of the red photographic light, designs came to life on the mummies' skin. Vertical stripes bearded the women's chins. On some, thin lines curved upward from their noses and dropped gracefully across their cheekbones. Lines arched and dipped over their eyebrows. Only the youngest woman and the two children had no tattoos. Scientists couldn't find any traces of the tattoos they knew some Inuit wore on their arms, legs, and hands.[5]

A PAINFUL ART

If you want a tattoo nowadays, you go to a tattoo artist's studio. There, the tattooist uses an electric needle gun to pierce tiny holes in your skin. As each hole is made, the needle deposits a small bit of tattoo ink. This ink is specially formulated to be nontoxic, or safe, for humans. Even with the quick-moving needle gun, getting a tattoo hurts, especially if it's on an area of skin that has many nerve endings, such as the face.[6]

The ancient Inuit didn't have modern-day tattoo technology. Instead, they created their body art using methods we consider primitive and unhealthy.

Most Inuit women used a sewing needle to make a tattoo. To begin, the tattooist threaded the needle with a thin piece of animal sinew. For the pigment, she coated the sinew thread with soot from the fire mixed with urine, preferably the urine of an old woman. Sometimes she used the juice from a special kind of seaweed. In later times, she may have used black gunpowder brought by visitors to the island.

One of the most complete descriptions of tattoo-making comes from Captain G. F. Lyon, who traveled with William Parry on one of his Arctic expeditions. In

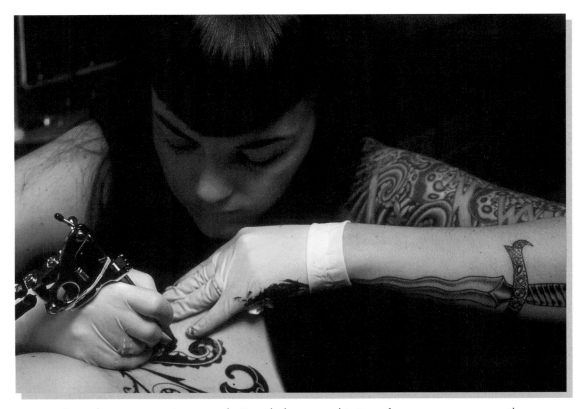

A modern tattoo artist at work. People have used tattoos for one reason or another for about 10,000 years. Tattoos are designed to be permanent. However, today most tattoos can be removed with lasers, but the procedure is usually costly.

1824, Parry's team visited the Inuit of the Hudson Bay area, a large inland sea in northern Canada. It was here that Lyon decided to have himself tattooed. In his journal, he described how an Inuit woman created his tattoo:

> *Having found a small needle, she took a piece of caribou sinew, which she blackened with soot. She began the work by sewing a rather deep but short stitch in my skin. When the thread was drawn beneath the skin, she pressed her thumb on the spot so as to press in the pigment. The next stitch commenced where the previous one ended. The work went slowly, for she broke a needle while trying to press it through my flesh. When she had sewed forty stitches and the stripe was about two inches long, I felt that it was enough. The operation ended with my skin being rubbed with whale oil.*

An Inuit woman also made tattoos by punching a small hole in the skin with a sharp, pointed tool we call an awl. Then she placed the tip of a thin, soot-covered needle into the hole. As she withdrew the needle, the tattooist held her fingertip over the hole to keep the pigment in place. The tattooed lines on Mummy 6 are an example of this method archaeologists call the dot technique.[7]

GOOD LUCK AND FAMILY TIES

If you've ever pricked yourself with a sharp needle, you can imagine how much it hurt to get a tattoo in the fifteenth century. The Inuit must have had very powerful reasons for enduring this kind of pain.

Those reasons differ from one Arctic region to the next. The customs differed, too. In most tribes, only Inuit women wore body and facial tattoos. In some tribes, both women and men wore them.

When Greenland was being colonized in 1721, the practice of tattooing started to disappear. It may have been the colonizers themselves who caused the practice to vanish. Many visiting priests considered tattooing barbaric and unwholesome, and discouraged the Inuit from doing it.

Often, it is unclear why the Inuit tattooed themselves, but before the practice died out completely, historians did learn many things about Inuit tattooing beliefs. When they interviewed the Inuit, the historians discovered that many tattooed themselves for superstitious reasons. One Canadian group believed tattoos helped a woman birthing a child. Some Inuit women said it made them skilled at their household tasks, while men felt tattoos guaranteed a successful hunt. Still others tattooed themselves out of fear—they believed that a woman who died without a tattoo risked having her skull used as a whale-oil lamp in the Land of the Dead.

There were other reasons, too. Beauty was one of them. Inuit women thought tattoos made them beautiful in the same way we think jewelry or a nice haircut does. They also used tattoos and other means to signal their marital status. A certain style of beadwork or the color of her hair ribbons or the style of her clothing told everyone if she was married or single.

Wearing a chin stripe tattoo was another way she signaled her marital status. In some Inuit groups, when a young girl became a woman, she had one stripe tattooed onto her chin. She added another when she married, and more for every child she bore. Scientists believe the youngest woman they discovered in the grave wore no tattoos because she hadn't married yet.

Some historians think that certain tattoo patterns originally showed family relationships. Mummies 5 and 8 have almost the same tattoos. Not only are the mummies close in age, but tests done on their skin tissue yielded identical results. Scientists believe the marks were the work of one artist and that the two women were sisters. Mummy 6's tattoos are so different that she may have come from a different tribe and may have married into the Qilakitsoq group.[8]

SIX

LAST DAYS

Like most cultures, people of the Arctic developed strong beliefs to explain why things happened the way they did. The Inuit didn't worships gods, but they did believe in a living force, or soul, called the inua. All living and nonliving things had this soul: rocks, mountains, plants, birds, animals, and humans. The inua was so powerful the people took their name from it, calling themselves Inuit in its honor.

The Inuit used inua to explain dreams, sickness, and death. During sleep, the inua traveled outside the body. This was the only time the inua could leave without harming it. If someone became sick, it meant the inua had been gone too long. If someone died, the inua had left for good.[1]

Not all inua were good, and the Inuit blamed bad things that happened to them on these wicked souls. Whenever possible, they tried to stay away from objects they thought were evil. If they felt that a sinister-looking pile of rocks intended mischief, they would walk miles out of their way to avoid it.

They also believed they could keep evil at bay if they used spells and amulets. A spell is a word or series of words that people sing or say. The Inuit believed these words had a magical effect and could ensure a successful hunt or turn away an attack of ghosts. The Inuit carried amulets with them wherever they went and often had many of them. A raven's beak, a small ivory statue, a dried flower, and a polar bear claw might be just a few of the amulets an individual carried to ward off evil.[2]

Sometimes, no matter how much magic they used, bad things still happened. People got lost. There were accidents. Mothers, fathers, and children got sick and sometimes died.

When someone died, that person traveled to the Land of the Dead, a strange and marvelous place inhabited by birds, fish, seals, and bears. Mermaids, monsters, and dragons lived there, too. Some of these creatures were very small and some were very large. Some were evil, and some were good or funny or kind.

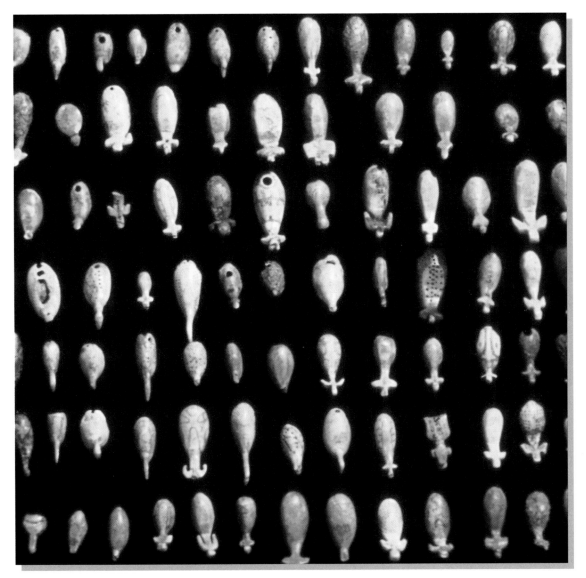

A collection of carved amulets

There were other supernatural powers the Inuit believed lived within them. When an Inuit died, the atiq, or name-soul, remained on earth, where it could haunt those who lived. To prevent this, no one could take the name of the dead person for a year or until a newborn baby was given the name. A person who shared the same name as the dead tribe member had to take a new one. If a tool or household item happened to have the same name as the dead person, tribe members renamed it.

The Inuit believed a long animal skin separated the Land of the Dead from the real world. To get there, the dead crawled beneath this skin. An adult made the journey in a year. Children traveled faster because they were smaller. As they traveled, the dead gradually shed their earthly fluids. To make their journey go more quickly, mourners tried not to cry, fearing that tears slowed their loved one's journey.[3]

AN EARTHLY EXPLANATION

Spiritual beliefs explained death to the Inuit, but scientists wanted a more earthly explanation. They wanted to know the physical details of how the Greenland mummies died.

Scientists knew the mummies lived about five hundred years ago, but carbon dating could only give an approximate time of death for each body. Did they die at the same time or at different times? If they died together, did an accident cause their deaths? Or did disease sweep through the tribe?

When scientists investigate how ancient people died, they first try to find out how healthy they were when alive. One way they find out is by performing an autopsy. An autopsy is the surgical opening of a dead person's body. It's usually performed by a pathologist, a doctor trained to identify diseases. A paleopathologist is a doctor who specializes in ancient diseases. Once he or she has opened up an ancient body, the paleopathologist can examine its organs for evidence of disease or poor nutrition.[4]

The investigators had already decided to do a complete medical exam on four of the most poorly preserved mummies. Nature had preserved the others so beautifully that they decided against performing an autopsy on them. Eventually, these mummies went back to Greenland, where they are on display at the Greenland National Museum.

The autopsy on Mummy 7 gave paleopathologists the best information about the state of her health. When they opened her body, scientists could see her lungs, heart, liver, gallbladder, stomach, and intestines. Though five hundred years in a stony arctic grave had hardened them, the organs still managed to tell the investigators a lot about her life.

Scientists could see that Mummy 7 had a healthy heart. Its four chambers and its coronary arteries showed no sign of disease. Her lungs told a different story. A black tarry substance, which the paleopathologists identified as soot, coated the inside of Mummy 7's lungs. The soot came from inhaling smoke from the whale oil lamp that always burned in an Inuit home.

When investigators opened Mummy 7's intestines, they found mummified feces. Feces is the waste matter the body produces and eliminates through the intestines. The scientists rehydrated, or added water, to the dark lump of feces and then dissected it. There they found small pieces of meat and animal hairs from seal, caribou, and arctic hares, along with small feathers and down from grouse and an arctic bird called an auk.

They also found lice eggs. Lice are parasitic, wingless insects that live on the hair and skin of humans, animals, and birds. They survive by sucking the blood of their hosts. Finding lice in Mummy 7's feces wasn't too surprising. Even today, some cultures consider lice a good source of food. Historical evidence shows this is true about the Greenland Inuit. Fabricius, a natural historian, wrote in 1780 that lice "thrive most abundantly on the heads and clothing of the Greenlanders . . . . They are eaten by the Greenlanders and considered delicious."

Scientists found evidence of lice infestation on Mummy 7 and on all the other mummies. Lice can easily move among people who share the same house, clothing, or bedding. They attach their eggs to hair follicles, and their bite can make the skin very itchy. Lice had laid eggs in Mummy 7's hair and on her clothing. Though lice were common in ancient Greenlanders, Mummy 7 had so many that scientists believe she may have been in poor health, making her vulnerable to a massive lice infestation.[5]

DISEASE OR ACCIDENT?

Life in Greenland five hundred years ago could not have been as easy as ours. The ancient Inuit didn't have the same advanced medical technology that we do. Diseases sometimes spread throughout the village, killing young and old alike.

During their examination, paleopathologists checked for signs of disease but could find no evidence that the eight Inuit had died from a contagious disease or from food poisoning. The investigators considered the possibility that the women and children had starved to death but quickly discarded that theory. Many of them still had evidence of fat beneath their skin. The fat would have disappeared if they had been starving. During famines, an extreme scarcity of food would have forced the Inuit to cut and boil strips of animal hide, which they would chew to soothe their raging hunger. Scientists found no chewed hides in or around the graves.

They next turned to the possibility that the eight Inuit died of a common accident. Perhaps, they considered, the women's umiak capsized in a boating accident. They would have died from drowning or exposure in the cold arctic sea. But the scientists could find no evidence of drowning. If the people had washed to shore after the accident, their clothing would have been filled with sand particles from the beach. And, as a modern-day Inuit told the scientists, their people would have buried them with the capsized boat.

It's possible the eight Inuit died separately. Scientists know the four-year-old boy had Down syndrome and that he may have died from complications associated with it. Down syndrome children sometimes die from heart disease or blood cancer. Mummy 8 may have died from her head cancer, but we can never be sure. We do know it made her blind in one eye and caused great pain.

X rays showed that Mummy 3 had a bone fragment in her intestinal tract. Scientists believe the sharp bone could have torn her gut. She would have died from the massive infection that usually follows such an accident. Since investigators decided against an autopsy on Mummy 3, we will never be sure what really caused her death.

To ensure that their dead lived comfortably in the Land of the Dead, the Inuit buried them with the tools and materials they used in their earthly lives. A man traveled with hunting equipment. A woman took things that she used for her domestic tasks, such as her sewing needle, a blubber lamp, her ulu. We call the things buried with people grave goods. The Greenland mummies' graves were filled with clothing, animal skins, and kamiks, which were meant to keep them warm in the afterlife.

Finally, scientists wanted to know why the six-month-old baby boy died, since their external investigation showed that he had been a healthy child. The answer to this question may lie in an ancient Inuit practice. When a mother died, the Inuit often killed her child or buried it alive with her. This is a horrible thing to think about, but

Mummy 8 was about fifty years old when she died of a malignant tumor.

in some Inuit societies of old, it was a necessity. In some tribes, there weren't enough people to take care of an orphan. The kindest thing its members could do was to allow the child to travel to the Land of the Dead with its mother. The child with Down syndrome may have been a victim of this same fate. Without the resources to care for such a handicapped child, the tribe may have found it easier to let him die.

We will probably never know how the Greenland mummies died, but science has told us much about how they lived. This, more than anything, helps us understand the ancient Inuit culture, one far removed from our own time and place.[6]

A.D. 982   Erik the Red, Norwegian Viking explorer, first arrives in Greenland.

1200   Norsemen and Inuit make contact with each other. The Norsemen called the Inuit "Skraellings," of whom they wrote, "They have no iron whatsoever and use walrus teeth for spears and sharp stones for knives."

1472/1473   Ships sent to Greenland by the Danish king Christian I are attacked by men in "small ships lacking keels, in great number."

ABOUT 1475   Six Inuit women and two children are buried at Qilakitsoq.

1576   Martin Frobisher leads an expedition to the Baffin Island area and reports that women of the island wear tattoos on their faces.

1577   John White, who participated in the Frobisher expedition, paints a watercolor showing a woman's tattoos.

1650s   Danish explorers capture an Inuit family. A Danish artist depicts them dressed in their fur clothing.

1700s	Russian fur traders cross the Bering Sea to the Aleutian Islands and Alaska, where they encounter the Aleuts. The traders over-hunt seals and sea otters and enslave or murder many Aleuts. By 1776, a majority of the 25,000 Aleuts are dead.
1900	A Scottish whaling ship brings disease to the Sadlermiut people of Southampton Island in Hudson Bay. The entire Sadlermiut population is wiped out.
OCTOBER 1972	Hans Grønvold discovers the Greenland mummies.
1977	Hans Grønvold travels to the Greenland Museum at Nuuk. There, Jens Rosing sees his photographs and realizes the significance of the discovery.
1978	Two scientific expeditions go to Qilakitsoq to retrieve the corpses and grave goods. Scientists perform autopsies on only four of the mummies.
1982	The four preserved mummies are sent back to the Greenland National Museum for display.

GLOSSARY

agloo   breathing hole made by seals and other sea mammals

Aleuts   native people from the Aleutian Islands, which is now part of Alaska

amputate   to cut off a part of the body

amulets   charms used to ward off evil

anesthetics   drugs that cause an insensitivity to pain

ante-mortem   before death

antibiotics   drugs used to destroy bacteria and other organisms

archaeologist   a scientist who studies the artifacts, inscriptions, and monuments left behind by ancient cultures

archer   a person who shoots with a bow and arrow

arthritis   inflammation of a person's joint

autolysis   the process of self-digestion

autopsy   the surgical opening of a body to look for causes of death and/or disease

awl   a pointed instrument used to punch holes in leather or wood

bacteria   microscopic organisms that cause disease and decay

bladder   a sac or organ that holds fluid or gas

calcium   a mineral that gives bones their strength

carbon dating   measures the amount of C-14 remaining in formerly living things; used to determine their age

caribou a large deer

char a kind of trout

clavicle collarbone

coronary arteries arteries that supply blood to the heart

dermis layer of skin below the epidermis

dissect to cut apart an animal or plant to examine its internal structure

Down syndrome a form of retardation that inhibits mental and physical development

enamel the hard outer covering of the tooth

enzymes organic substances that originate from living cells

epidermis the outer layer of skin

Eskimos name formerly used to designate the Inuit

feces waste material discharged through the intestines

fjord a long, narrow arm of the sea bordered by steep cliffs

flense to strip the blubber and skin from a whale or other sea creature

forensic anthropologist a scientist who studies the minute details of the human skeleton

frostbite frozen, formerly living tissue

furrow a groove

gangrene a dangerous infection that occurs when tissue dies from lack of blood

garment a piece of clothing

gut intestines

harpoon a barbed spear attached to a rope and thrown

igloo a temporary Inuit shelter made from blocks of snow

infestation a troublesome overrun of destructive animals

infrared photography a photographic technique that reveals things hidden beneath the epidermis

inni an Inuit word for igloo

inua a soul, or life force, the Inuit believed inhabited all things

Inuit the People

kamiks boots made of skin

kayak   a single-person boat made of a frame and skin covering

lice   tiny, wingless parasitic animals

nontoxic   safe for humans

ossify   to turn to bone

pack ice   large area of ice covering the northern seas in winter

pact   an agreement

paleopathologist   a scientist who studies the nature, origin, and course of disease in the bodies of ancient humans

parka   a winter jacket

pelvis   cradle of bone located between the hips

permafrost   a permanent layer of frozen ground

pigment   coloring

pollinate   to transfer pollen to the stigma of a flower, used by plants to reproduce themselves

putrefaction   decomposition of organic matter by bacteria and other organisms

rehydrate   to add water

sinew   a thick band of tissue that connects muscles to bone

sod   a section cut from grassland or tundra

spells   magic words or phrases

subterranean   below ground

supraorbital ridge   ridge of bone located over the eyes

sutures   places where the plates of the skull join together

tattoo   a decoration made beneath the skin

thimble   a protective covering for a finger; used in sewing

tundra   vast, treeless plains located in the arctic regions

ulu   a curved knife

umiak   a round skin boat

urine   a liquid waste product excreted by the kidneys

ventilate   to provide a room with fresh air

vertebrae   the bones of the spine

virus   an organism that causes disease

S O U R C E   N O T E S

ONE : A STONEY GRAVE

1. Personal Interview with Hans Grønvold, (August 1996).

J. P. Hansen, J. Meldgaard, J. Nordqvist, *The Greenland Mummies*. (Washington, D.C.: Smithsonian Institution Press 1991), 39–52.

J. P. Hansen, J. Meldgaard, J. Nordqvist, "The Mummies of Qilakitsoq." *National Geographic*, February 1985, 191–207.

2. Personal Interview with Hans Grønvold (1996).

Hansen, Meldgaard, Nordqvist, *The Greenland Mummies*, 39–52.

Hansen, Meldgaard, Nordqvist, "The Mummies of Qilakitsoq," 191–207.

3. Hansen, Meldgaard, Nordqvist, *The Greenland Mummies*.

Hansen, Meldgaard, Nordqvist, "The Mummies of Qilakitsoq."

4. Douglas Ubelaker and Henry Scammell, *Bones: A Forensic Detective's Casebook*. (New York: Edward Burlingame Books, 1992), 86–104.

Wm. R. Maples and Michael Browning, *Dead Men Do Tell Tales*. (New York: Doubleday,1994).

Hansen, Meldgaard, Nordqvist, *The Greenland Mummies*, 49–51.

5. Ibid.

TWO : A STORY IN THE BONES

1. Jane McIntosh, *The Practical Archaeologist: How We Know What We Know About The Past*. (New York: Facts on File, 1986), 117.

2. *Science and Technology Illustrated*. (Chicago: Encyclopaedia Britannica. Gruppo Editoriale Fabbri), 3538–3540.

3. Hansen, Meldgaard, Nordqvist, *The Greenland Mummies*, 66–81.

55

4. Douglas Ubelaker, and Henry Scammell, *Bones*, 86–104.

5. Hansen, Meldgaard, Nordqvist, *The Greenland Mummies*, 68.

6. Robert Berkow, ed. *The Merck Manual, Sixteenth Edition*. (Rahway, NJ: Merck Research Laboratories, 1992), 2248, 2260.

7. Ibid.

Hansen, Meldgaard, Nordqvist, *The Greenland Mummies*, 68.

8. Douglas Ubelaker and Henry Scammell, *Bones*, 86–104.

9. Hansen, Meldgaard, Nordqvist, *The Greenland Mummies*.

10. Ibid.

THREE : ANCIENT ARCTIC DWELLERS

1. Hansen, Meldgaard, Nordqvist, *The Greenland Mummies*, 15–36.

Kevin Osborn, *People of the Arctic*. (New York: Chelsea House, 1990), 13–16.

2. Ibid.

3. Ibid.

4. Barry Lopez, *Arctic Dreams*. (New York: Charles Scribner's Sons, 1986), 21–23.

Joseph Wallace, *The Arctic*. (New York: Gallery Books, 1988), 10–25.

5. Hansen, Meldgaard, Nordqvist, *The Greenland Mummies*, 151–160.

Wallace, *The Arctic*.

6. Kaj Birket-Smith, *Eskimos*. (Norman, Oklahoma: University of Oklahoma Press, 1988), 51–58.

7. Ibid.

8. Osborn, *People of the Arctic*, 36–46.

9. Lopez, *Arctic Dreams*, 196.

FOUR : KEEPING WARM

1. Hansen, Meldgaard, Nordqvist, *The Greenland Mummies*, 117–149.

2. Lopez, *Arctic Dreams*, 191.

3. Hansen, Meldgaard, Nordqvist, *The Greenland Mummies*, 117–149.

Lopez, *Arctic Dreams*, 191–192.

4. Ibid.

5. Birket-Smith, *Eskimos*, 41–49.

Hansen, Meldgaard, Nordqvist, *The Greenland Mummies*, 117–149.

6. Ibid.

7. Ibid.

8. Osborn, *People of the Arctic*, 70–75.

9. Birket-Smith, *Eskimos*, 48–49.

FIVE : TATTOOS—INUIT BODY ART

1. Lopez, *Arctic Dreams*, 188–189.

2. Osborn, *People of the Arctic*, 77–94.

3. Hansen, Meldgaard, Nordqvist, *The Greenland Mummies*, 103–115.

4. *Science and Technology Illustrated.*

5. Hansen, Meldgaard, Nordqvist, *The Greenland Mummies*, 103–115.

6. Personal interview with tattoo artist John Dunn. (August 1996).

7. Hansen, Meldgaard, Nordqvist, *The Greenland Mummies*, 103–115.

8. Ibid.

SIX : LAST DAYS

1. Hansen, Meldgaard, Nordqvist, *The Greenland Mummies*, 55–63.

2. Birket-Smith, *Eskimos*, 89–108.

3. Hansen, Meldgaard, Nordqvist, *The Greenland Mummies*, 55–63.

4. Don Brothwell, *The Bog Man and the Archaeology of People*. (Cambridge, MA: Harvard University Press, 1986) 64–67.

5. Hansen, Meldgaard, Nordqvist, *The Greenland Mummies*, 55–63.

6. Ibid.

FURTHER READING

Birket-Smith, Kaj. *Eskimos*. Norman, Oklahoma: University of Oklahoma Press, 1988.

Brothwell, Don. *The Bog Man and the Archaeology of People*. Cambridge, MA: Harvard University Press, 1987.

Hansen, J. P., J. Meldgaard, J. Nordqvist. *The Greenland Mummies*. Washington, D.C.: Smithsonian Institution Press, 1991.

Hansen, J. P., J. Meldgaard, J. Nordqvist. "The Mummies of Qilakitsoq." *National Geographic*, February 1985, 191–207.

Lopez, Barry. *Arctic Dreams*. New York: Charles Scribner's Sons, 1986.

Maples, Wm. R. and Michael Browning. *Dead Men Do Tell Tales*. New York: Doubleday, 1994.

McIntosh, Jane. *The Practical Archaeologist: How We Know What We Know About The Past*. New York: Facts on File, 1986.

Osborn, Kevin. *People of the Arctic*. New York: Chelsea House Publishers, 1990.

Science and Technology Illustrated. Chicago: Encyclopaedia Britannica. Gruppo Editoriale Fabbri, 1983.

Siska, Heather Smith. *People of the Ice: How the Inuit Lived*. Buffalo, NY: Firefly Books, 1992.

Ubelaker, Douglas and Henry Scammell. *Bones: A Forensic Detective's Casebook*. New York: Edward Burlingame Books,1992.

Wallace, Joseph. *The Arctic*. New York: Gallery Books, 1988.

I N D E X

ABOUT THE AUTHOR

Janet Buell is an elementary school enrichment teacher. Her main interests are anthropology, archaeology, reading, soccer, and softball. The time she spent exploring a local bog made her want to find out more. In her research, she discovered the existence of bog bodies and other ancient humans. It soon turned into the idea for this book series.

Janet was born and raised in Illinois and now lives in Goffstown, New Hampshire.